EVOLVING DRINKS WHICH PENGUINS RECALL

EVOLVING DRINKS WHICH PENGUINS RECALL

poems

L. Blume

TALL ISLAND PRESS
New York, New York

FIRST EDITION

Cover art: Emporer penguins in the Southwest Ross Sea. (Courtesy of Michael Van Woert, NOAA NESDIS, ORA)

Book & Cover Design: Christine Holbert, Lost Horse Press: www.losthorsepress.org

Tall Island Press
PO Box 1943
New York, NY 10013

ISBN-13: 978-0991327201
ISBN-10: 0991327209
LCCN:2013958176

for Remus

CONTENTS

EVOLVING DRINKS WHICH PENGUINS RECALL

DOZE ZEE DOTE ZEN DOWN

What if you danced on an altered molecular surface
or a hilltop unto itself
and anonymity, instinct and personal scrap
transposed a certain reality into a foggy night
stretched down to zip
and nobody noticed?

THE INSOLUBLE DEWDROP (I)

Deliciously icky
the flying fiasco came standard
beating the fog off the morning line.

And then we set out to find nicknames.
With our penlights blazing
it was a totem struggle.

THE MORNING FOG OF SOLVATION (II)

Guided by our penlights
we watched the neon-clad monks
escape and go digital.

They sat in techno bliss
breaking code and stacking wooden blocks
mindful that nature will be looted
by the serious hobbyist.

Diligently repairing our nicknames
in a frenzy of simple text
we picnicked a wave-height apart.

Who is a cat?
To solve that, we screamed.
Screaming—whoever imagined?

Sure, it was easy enough
for fueling the cafe
snowfall and all.

WHERE THERE ARE NO MONSTERS

(ONLY A TENSE DISPASSION OF THE FROZEN VARIETY)

It's a hard jump.
Try to go through
and bring treats.

Edge to squash
and down without a copilot
the frogs rumbled along.

For the worm was glued to the paper
oblivious that it had been
dumped in the soil.

Stuttering in light of the stars
the thrill was in the gibberish.
How muddy.

TO GO BACK TO GO THROUGH

The light of the multiverse
spread like a dusky wave
rolling around the end of an echo
and through a narrow crack.

In the short term
the future is hard to unknot.
Slowly it will become less stiff
and fall back.

By a slip of the brain
you land in the denominator
miscible with the filmy layer
of lightly floured hands
feeling repacked.

WE'VE HEARD COMPLAINTS

We saw the mango madness
in motion—a microcosm
essentially barren, hustled in vain
and riding the juicy tentacle
of reality—but still managed to put
fairly safe food on the table.

A QUARTER OF, TOO

Overhead, the cries of microorganisms
circling the vast highlands
created sheepfolds of anxiety.

Most of all, they appeared off-slant
banging into feathers and infesting the rain.
It is microbiology on a kite string.

Reverse engineering, we wondered
how to retile the grand illusion.
Clearly it is an uneven bisection.

OFURO ET FOGGERS

Stuck on the iffiest roller coaster
Jill pounded anxiety
into cast-iron coolness.

You have to admire her outlook.
Darker than a double-bass bow
with age it will be jet-black.

FROM WHAT YOU ARE RUNNING FROM

Sorry gang.
I accidentally struck out.

The same disclaimer is posted
on the back of the serum.

INTERJECTING GRAVITY, COAXING INERTIA AND OTHER IMPROBABLE PHENOMENA TOUCHING A CRAZY IMAGINATION

Elusively aspheric
and symbolized in one bite
we connected hand to back
to protect the outside wrapper

Although optically unexpected
without leaning on chop psychology
the limber act worked
at least on the label.

WHACKED
(A JOLT OF JULY)

Playing hardball
with judo-thrown accuracy
the mallet met the sandbox.
Wham.

Batter up.

EXTRAPOLATE THAT

A ting, a twang and a thud
tossed into the rising agitation
in a quagmire played out
and juxtaposed with
an amalgam of anomalies.

Despite the falling-out
distance between us
our belly buttons bumped.
We decided to move back
so as not to
interrupt the bagpipers.

AT THE FIRST POINT

You are uncertain
that you heard the big bang
but you know the rest

long questions
one after another
rippling supple notes.

UNGLUED

Swamped and full of pitfalls
with some rot in the center
some rust on the wing bands
and some loose bits for hanging emphasis
it was still an attractive bargain.

Dirt falling off the body
was a step toward self-cleaning
baring the unknown.

Along its far side
you sink affably
and listen to the mass wasting.

MEDICAL MOCHA

The fateful sip
let the predator in the tunnel
each drop hotwiring the melon patch
until the shaking began.

A CROSS-WORDED QUARTET

Gosh shimmy joshed merrily.
Joshed merrily gosh shimmy.

Monaural and with a lot of hiss
Joni could not get her kilter on.

THE UNPLINKABLE

Dropped in a riveting, prograding,
crow-licking, dry-hopping
splash
the test tube burst.

Come teatime
you cringe, tug, tumble,
sell, join hands
and pour bourbon.

HANG ON

The honk meter
recorded a whooshing ride
as you flamed and thrashed
in a twisted orbit.

Accelerating through
the cycle of fourths
you traded lisp-for-lisp
with the fat bulldog.

Parked in a deformed decade
you hand calculated
a rough and itchier trend
attributed to magical snooping.

Toward bedtime
snouts reverberated.

SKYLAB IN THE HOOD

A squeezy armrest
wider at the pumping end
took the tension out of the winding.

Hung slack
the rubber seam reinforced
its snap.

Strained in an open pose
flailing
you removed the safety net
and stretched the jib.

SPLICING THE VACANT SPOTS

The last rover
came to a soft stop
and stood cold.

In the attic
a trunkful of action figures
sat among the cobwebs.

I was concerned by all of this
but you operate strictly on the basis
that the rip current will run its course.

Amplified ear to ear
and strumming your mop banjo style
sure put a good scare in motion.

RITUAL HORTICULTURE

I am still wearing the green shadow
made from seaweed and slime
that I gardened with a wrinkled stick.

Is it bug-infested?
No, not yet.
It is still larval.

Tofu rehash.
Yes, I tried it once.
It tasted a bit bland
but it would have been a waste
to throw it to pasture.

STAINED PAST TINGED

Rattled down and fully exposed
her hot breath
beat down on your scapegoat skin.

It was the tipping point
as a tailwind of wisdom
broke under suction

and facets
joined frost to frost
began to melt

spring-releasing
more than a life sty.

HEARING EVIL AND SEEING ROAST BEETS

Having flirted with
past spies and present lies
you lean around the flagpole
and ponder the wrecking ball
with its dangling gentility.

MYNA

Working up an unsweetened
response to a pesky trill

you lay down a
tonally buttressed
bass-clef twist

crocodile-solid and dithered
with an eyeball-wrenching groove.

BEBOP OR BE LATE

Blank and on the brink of bliss
I changed the pitch
to yellow, low
and aggressive

and tinkered
with the rhythm
to produce
a famous last revision.

Scurrying uphill
and over the grade
I spotted a flock
of wintering thrushes.

Hearing their calls
I struggled to integrate
their mantra.
It sure was loud.

SYNCHRONIZING A TIME SPIRAL

As relaxing as it was
sitting against the wall
deodysseyfying
we were over the limit.

Striding away
we churned up the flip view
of a boundless past
to get to either side of luck.

WEIGHING THE MIGHTIEST

Facing pleasant and unpleasant conversations
circular passages
and 10 tons of glowing steel
was less than
a shake-the-woodwork adventure.

But we digress.

WORKSCREW

Out on a mission
probing the origin of ambition
we topped off in a high gear

only to discover
many expectations
on the cutting-room floor.

As we descended
the steps
a squeaky vibrato

unnaturally stiff
but in the right way
supported the workload.

IDIOSYNCHRONOUS

You point up.
A hummingbird box
the size of a small housefly
vibrates.

October, a sword-fighting wonder
corrupts the vibes
striking an opinionated riddle.

Ding-dong.
Darwin enters
attracting a curled range of life.

The snailplows slide close
with erratic adjustments.
Their ductility distorts
your luminous thread.

Simultaneously a clean spell replicates
and chops up your coda
with a large amount of voodoo.

Your thoughts avalanche
microinterpreting the burn marks
of nails driven in for support.

Outside the sky rings clear.
The snailplows worry you.

INTRODUCING TOMORROW

Juggling beauty and fame
bionic Barbara sneered
and slurred a slightly nasal phrase.

Tess responded
by straddling a loaded point
and chirping a tense vocabulary.

The action strengthened
the artificial muscles
covering her bare precepts.

Kindling the flipside
Rick and Laura repeatedly
poked the flames with chisels.

Fun aside
evening came.

FOOLSHED

Bragging of the white gnat
and where it slurps

Sylvia edged over
and harpooned my heart.

Hers expanded.
Ah, more room.

THE MYSTICALLY HEARD SCREAMS OF BUSHMEAT

The questions matched
but our wishes varied.

Using light-headed logic
we realized our dream
to create a bubble.

Naturally it burst
and the prophets adjourned.

Barely level, we expected a challenge.
Go, they said.

Trembling hands repeatedly raised an anthem
shaping a vision that whispered
don't cry lamb, stupid monkeys.

As our brains navigated the dustbin
we stalled.

Reduced to forgery
our earnings were printed
in a washing machine.

Pending a multivariate irrational walk
we tore down a wall of loans.

Like the emotional battle
of fools sputtering in the dark
our wisdom burned precariously.

THE HANDBAG, DEAR

The protest crushed
the main point wrinkled
and Kara's handbag turned upside down.

Ignoring the rain
she fled wearing the wrong foot.
Ouchy.

DIRTY SHIRT OFF

Potent cranes pulsed tirelessly up
up into obstacles
hitting uncommon number densities
when the prevalent garment applied.

While applying rough prerequisites
T invited the entire tactile anatomy.
She considered long names unattached
potentially penetrating the I = U.

Clair, atop Wendell, read in distraction.
She sought brief paragraphs
distilling swift points.

Alison poured fractional discipline.
The procedure produced tall islands
distant places
Scotland
pulp dunes, upside bones.

WONDER WOMAN

Everything looked wrong.
A test sequence, unfolding, had collapsed.
Various side groups pointed deeply to the southeast.
And then she said in low voice, research on.

Around strains of car horns
formal in tone control
but sparse in tensile root
vessels trickled backward
and we moved left.

Report, she said.
We reported oh-so-superior
colorful trees of oceans
a laughing effect
and applauded passionately.

SPIDER LEAD CRYSTALLIZED

1 Surprise!
Ethel always seemed shrewd
though profound
more code than pace
spinning around open anomalies
in top form.

2 Impudent convoys
Wednesday was kind
unlike those browsers
who aspired to all-out use of time
chance-shifted off lofty halls
recently called academic.

3 Initiative
Move a mood
hence a lifetime.
Provoke fortitude, darling.
Chronicle the diffuse unfamiliar dimension.
Appear important.

4 Clever dirt
Dorothy awakened attired
in artificial common knowledge
absurd capacity
complex technical blocks
recognized as tomorrow's obvious assessment.

THE METER LAPSED

Pump, pull, crudely shape the stuff
the ether vacuum where spoon talked.
Cleopatra's needle withdrew
and I was safe.

Dimly smiling, I pedaled past
crystal liquid
intoxicated telephony
coffee
rich fossils
alone or highly distorted.

I fixed distance, heard my
name, record
name, record
name, record
name . . .
Pretend to run.
Pedal.

Far from acquired motions
familiarized into prayers of repeating literature
positions tuned the senses below colorful notes
untied tightly into prolonged time
up or down

THE LOOM OF PERPLEXITY

Helen accepted the curl
dented, withdrawn, changed
by the coconut into one pattern
that tied the ends of the paradox.

HURRICANE GLORIA'S PULSE

A chorus of sunlight
shouted with arms in the sky
communicated high-spirited misfortune.

HIDE AND SHAKE

Clara pulled and out came the secret.
One times one is exciting.

PASS THE COMPASS

Having paid for innovation
we compiled the unknown
instigating memories inside corners of the circuit.
The output activated large-named chemicals
equalizing the average current decay
and position of thick, picturesque conductors.
Comparing the end to the model
the machine handled the preconstruction
compressing and folding capacity
as the fabric hardened.
Quietly, we accelerated the box
satisfied that we had received direction.

EVOLVING DRINKS WHICH PENGUINS RECALL

Besieged on high ground
far above the tree floor
programs spun fruitless code
as we wondered
what had ruined our analysis.
And all protested
that man houses carelessness
while others whispered, not her.
Noses, nevertheless, ended positively close
completely beloved
sparsely eternal.

IN MEMPHIS

Being kind, the handsome spy
verified that the disputed file
had been attached to something prohibited.
Beatrice, startled by the virulence it expressed
canceled her desire.

YOU, OVER THERE

The Queen, who is hard,
has been less crowded
since she discovered that life's collisions
return as elastic spheres
the size of the average eight-horsepower person.

PASSING TIME

I pick up the music and begin to play.
The eight interpretations
and the allied lines flow optimistically.
Hammered, rolled and balanced by silence
the gist of both sticks operated skillfully
continues in a spontaneous way.
Quickly beautiful, the theme races ahead
hidden in part and profoundly blooming
before withdrawing.
I wander about and start to lose interest.
G repeats.

THE PLACE

I am in the garden
looking at the delay.
The veins are not open.
Is it possible to add furniture?

WILD TOMATOES

You lost them.
I found them.
Catherine painted them.

Inspired by a deep sense
that she had had fun
Eve said that she felt them.

PROJECT REVIEW

Z observed that relationships
cannot be locked with bolts.
Screw buttons, perhaps.

SEA SHOCK

The snow turned off
hiding the coastline behind
a wall of sour precipitation.

Graffitied rabbits soon appeared on the bluff
shifting into columns
and keeping the decimal afloat.

Stop.
The movement is slower.

The light is soft, bright and dangerous
and billows like water flowing upbeat
and ruffled on top.

It is not distinct
but divides and satisfies
like plotting discretion versus success.

The vision had passed in length
too obscured to catch sight of the textured parts
late details, blobs double-faulting on and on
threading in a circus or two.

Eventually it became clear
that Marilyn had spoken.

TOSSED EMOTION

Suppose Annie declined
sent you a detailed past
gave you a concealed turnoff
a slow, viscous surprise.

EXCEEDING SUSTAINABILITY

He is not in love with the petroleum-powered horse.
Free energy is simply a physical concept.

IN PHASE

Burning brightly
the Sun passed

wrapping the land
in a tinted stream

of tangled tones
guaranteed by the hour

which seemed noble
but expensive.

GOING AWAY COMES BACK

Charged under false ionization
the air expanded and jumped to a colder altitude
where particles grew
icy substrates splendid and clear
and droplets gurgled and bolted
dissolving the clouds in a flash
which rained on the dogtrot.

DREAM LOUDLY

If you agree with the skeptics
there is no possibility of danger
in the natural world.

But what if there is no next year?

Take a shot of the alternative fuel
replace your mind's left display
and economize.

FREEWHEELING

Hold the string.
Its petals seem deranged.

If you mash the flow
it will be angry.

Fill up on the myth
that roars from the box.

Please stop casting stripes.
Instead, sprinkle a bag of wiggles.

Apply capacitance in difficult threes.
Excavate four cycles.

Turn a joule of idiocy
into a cryogenic thrill.

And fetch the lifeboat.

THE NORTH LESS

A collapsed chunk of the Arctic
slipped in line with the overall ecology.

Behind the buffered silence
you guess the temperature skipped a foot.

You put on the breaks to think.
Taking the train is easier than walking.

DOWNTIME

I've never tried kendo
or any other stick sports.

But dialing the galaxy's
low frequency seems familiar.

Its capacity to absorb quantum stress
stops the excitement from eroding.

TOUCH BLIND

Blind to the motion of the brush
you encrypt the mural with a crease.

You must have a strong curiosity
to crash and boom.

As a friend or close equivalent
you argue that things rarely change upward.

Electronic cities tend to be a pile of cubes
trapped characteristically way too close.

Hesitating to give meaning at face value
you give thanks on behalf of many.

QUARRYING

Every night the star sinks south.
It is destined to be cool.
Adjusting the friction of its string might cut its drag
and balance the loads to match its stiffness
but that cannot stop the repetition
or dissolve the amber veil once its band gap expands.
The Earth has a similar crustiness
where new is brand-new soft green moss
and old is just brown dust.

HOPING PART A WILL FIT

I've often thought of the vast reserves
left on most days, of oversize footprints,
invisible spheres, countercurrent whirlpools,
ethereal downspouts, of Hannah adjusting her dress.
I've also observed that the voltage is higher
in the left pulse beat and that Cairo has an appealing
magenta silence an octave above the path often taken.

POGO ON TWIN CONGAS

A clear layer of notes echoed the beat
drummed with a sawed-off broom.

The song trembled around the divine tree
enchanting us into a new tribalism.

As we leapt around the wood god
they gave us a gong.

Bang!

The silken gray moonset
splintered into scorching bicolor tulips.

Thrown off-scale
we played on.

When the raga strum lands
it can really make you sit down.

FIXED IN TIME

Side 1 was a crushing blow.

For 32 years, Kathryn's methodological conscience
devoured various thoughts
until her deductive power source stumbled.

The wind could not shake
her dose-craving dependence.
It was too deep to bottle.

One small structure
contrasted her multihued problem
of limitless movement
thrown in with mathematics
on long blackboards.

Dividing the principle it decorated
was a questionable use of the numbers.
But when read lengthwise
it was a safe lesson.

Side 2 held a small bird's note.

PEEKING THROUGH A STAND OF BAMBOO

The human genome shed its heredity on level eight
which was wide, red and too intense to takeoff on.

Antifriction pangs rippled
yanking apart my imagination.

To compensate for the accumulated torsion
a friendly dog chewed the frayed remains.

Psycho-empirical evidence suggests
that the opposite leaf of the medulla
connects the line that discharges ridicule.

It is a family characteristic
as is unicycling on ice.

Sensing the trap that shrews jump over
I consumed the antidote.

SCREAMLINER

With inflated zest
Irene blended exponents
bisected proofs
shook-up fractions
shuffled fine addition
tripped-off patterns
compiled junk
and outwitted intuition
for overtaking a high-speed train.

TO SHINE

Ignited in the starlight
the shining stones
tricked me into a fantasy
where every excuse is urgent.

A sweet deception emerged
packed with more lumens per hour.
Struggling to economize
I caught the plot drifting.

Smoke and secret dispersions
bent the incandescence
whose intensity was brighter
the second the tuba paused.

I enjoyed a delicate moment in the light
until a thin sawing voice trilled.
It was better to ignore this
since steering the mind, honestly, is harder.

BULLDOZING ENTHUSIASTS

Jackie channeled Jacob's flow
mobilizing a raft of dark energy
that accelerated faster than the river.
Cosmic wonder, you said.

As revolving policyholders of the magic wand
they requested spots of reactive gas
sorbed inside the green tube
to balance the day-before function.

For Jackie, the charm was in the morning.
She got up and mined the joke machine
but was surprised when the backcourt of the Arctic
tore its skin off the sphere so fast that it hurt.

Jacob, whose magic is indifferent
ate a little, rested
and passed through the electric current.
His monopolar-connected lines
altered an abridged kinesis
strengthened by reseeding the boreal backyard.

You take a hypnotic breather
and dismount the D train
feeling more sympathetic for the Earth.
Small wonder, they said.

BOLSHEVILLE

The red eyes of dawn hung over
shored-up rickety theories,
the kind that are old
and tend to be spit out.

With detached fascination
I chased an expired memory of Sophia
reciting the solution in a tipsy climax.
Cheers cascaded.

As for my whimsies
they tend to end as a waste of insanity.
Nevertheless, I took a sip of the binary meditation
and detected a hint of Lila.

The bulk of my remaining output
emitted piece by piece
was reanimated with the feeling of a willow bed
hinged endurably at theta.

I lay down an ace.
It reflected to some extent
the hyper state of a young synapse
in an agile world that no longer defines me.

SHE WHO BETS THE FISH HITS TENDERNESS

A gloved fate underlying the embers
awakened the suture and wrenched open a rift
venting and rupturing the cocoon.

Rhythmic winds swirled further inward
smashing and rotating the spiked count backward
over arcs magnified and folded off-center.

The sky's plunging hail count
coated, melted and purified the earth
as the passing thunder dampened and ended.

Moving in the form of a yawn
a breeze aroused the scents of rain
and blooms—summer.

The exaggerated spectacle
linked the ideal locale, Eden, pirates,
merry fruit, the debility of it all.

Still, the world maintained its curvature.

WORKING TOO MUCH

Surfacing where the expectation is dug
you shout and drop a nut.
It is a competent deviation of behavior
and harmless show of importance.

Convinced from a position of weatherized renewal
the others fall cold and monkey quietly.
You adjust the horizontal
and their tilt slips away.

Brooklyn, you insist, is adopted.
It is the arch, cagier house
populated by those who agree
that noise logically accompanies social technology.

You yearn to attach a rope to the proton
and pull the others past the calm promontory
of wastefulness to where the bay accelerates
and elasticity resides stuffed in boxes.

Laughing, you reach the peak super-separated
and enamored by the fringe abnormities.
It is very quiet.
The openness makes the photograph look hungry.

RECTIFYING THE VAGRANCY OF LICHEN

Part hammer, part Dionysian discord
L ricocheted, expired, healed, proved part hen
and broke up charged hopping waves.

Spaced outta here
her forehead
hit the anesthetizing button.

The rock-bottom intensity gauge
thawed her relentless pace
producing either giggling prostrations or fallen gin fits.

Spot-checking her unverified deeds
under the lingering smoke
J threw L a snorkel.

THE LARKED INDUCTION
OF COAXIAL HERITAGE ON TAP

Soon after we crossed the straw bridge
the sound of rust eating the forest
became an indistinct, fragmentary murmur.

A denticulated magnet knelled red.
It was equal and clear.
Overreacting, we feared the faint blue nervousness.

We withstood it in this way:
a spot, a step, a pack of diodes
and a pledge of gore.

The exquisite side of the clock
rattled the oboe's voice
dampening its mood and obstructing our celebration.

In the course of the dodecahedral octave
we grieved those incriminated
by the achromatic omen.

Bewailing our digested musings
the scythe and chimes
squeezed out a maniacal refrain.

PROVING THE RADIUS OF CONCENTRATION

Traveling to the end
the spittle gently combined
and finally stopped.

Emilia used her beam
as spending power.
Its powerful chutes spent.

Her links degenerated.
And although conscious
she was less sharp.

The ample flower garland has lived in pain.
It barely seemed capable of melting the dew.
But the bamboo reached its goal.

Licking the ashtray an inch
and then salivating
is a serious problem.

AN ILL-HUMORED NANONOCTURNE

Carrying a positive rotation
you entered the opening of a pantomime.
At best it was an escape,
a wild fall off the fence.

On fire and reeling in the wake
of the a sine wave
you obtained a high level of joy
from a minimum of whiskey.

Biting both sides of the mixture
turned a sea of negative numbers into a huge hole.
Perhaps it was too loud an explosion.
Feeling the sting, you exhaled.

Sitting on the bus
added to the puzzle
as winter flew away
the seashore floated loose
and the night passed.

ADAPTING

Suppose that's it
the stitch is done
overwritten as a blank surprise
a computable dead end
that wilts and moves the handle.

Suppose the jellyfish lost its head
the capsular structure
protecting the junk-built theory
of the instinctual front door.

Suppose it's her thing
to dabble in a lace inferno
disguised as an arbitrary weave.

Tonight the lions are in touch
breathing full throttle.

A SACK OF RATIONAL ANXIETY

Clearing the path
little by little
the notion to run away
escaped Alyssa.

On the other side
of the present-day Bronx
a dormant bone struck
for the second time.

Jamming before the underground twins
her snippet of inspiration
played back as an uneven impulse.

It intensified naturally
when the subfield
wove a clear wavefront.

In search of green
and not yet armed
a close friend
wearing a clay mask
cracked.

TO FACE THE FAUCET KNOWING THAT IT IS DRY (NOT EVEN A DRIBBLE)

A pile of leaves
arranged in a winding array
continued as a low-pressure system
to the left side of the table
wiping out characters, unity,
muffins and half of your brain
leaving the wow.

You sit believing that the room is bending
with its glossy geometry
and mix of 10 cymbals
heard at bat volume.

Jumping back to view
the fruit and honeycomb
you connect the math.
He has changed.
His behavior is amber-colored
in the shape of a porridge.

Emotions calmed
the footlights dimmed
and sound of kitty tied to the bell rose
in protest to the sudden enthusiasm
of the delivery person
collecting fish in the rain.

NIBBLING TENDER PEARS
AND WISHING AWAY THE WINTRY DEW

Empty but fiery enough
you lead a life of sighs and ashes.

You appreciate the subunits
the boo-boos of history
and blurs of the day.

Water wears out things
and constructs your future.

You sprinkle an effective amount
and notice that a single flower is beautiful
just for the lazy bones that it is.

SPELUNKING FIRES UP A PHOBIA

A prisoner by wisdom of the scorpion
and careful of all toxic species
I took a curious trip through Ana's universe.

It hosted the fragile quanta
of a chic yin and quacked yang
leaving her to invest in the appropriate
force to grow Seattle.

Reasoning in a neutral hew
for lack of breakfast
she laughed in hyena.

Her response proved to be
a margin wider than a fingertip
provided that the Caribbean spirits were parallel.

A LINEAR CHANGE OF LUCK

Almost every inanimate object
such as an oil slick
on the surface of a puddle
is irrelevant.

The tree, however, is in excellent condition
with only two loose parts
and a degree of firmness greater than zero.

Short of the large kind
the most gorgeous fruit
on its branches are small.

Medium-sized tufts of mutual purpose
come from its leaves.
There are lots of them.

STRANGE AND COMPLEX RUBY WITHOUT HESITATION

Dusting off a turnip
you are inclined to remain solid.

A line spray-painted on it
was looming yet vanishing enough.

The counter netting tingled
but that was easy to stop.

Thirsty, you came in from the dark
knocked back four fears

and pressed a favorable turn of the grid
full force and on track, for sure.

WALKING IN THE ANTICLINE

Toggling in my sleep
an idea floated
that caused the earth to acquire a slip.

Bushwhacked?
You bet.
Rephrased, it deformed.

Unfurling her inner zip
Alex extended a black olive.

It was the stimulus
of a powerful jones
fast and smooth.

Traveling by taxi
inertia carried us
seven seats into the arcade.

Clinging to the frost
I am optimistic that we are not elves.

But in a pool of more than one stone,
with two halves moving forward
it is hard to focus on a third.

THE STUFF WE CRAVE IS IMITATION

Line-forming light segments
squirted out a sequel

where we are excited, mad,
sort of vague and stuck in a comical plane.

Meanwhile a frictionally intoned moo
in a diminished mode

scaled the notes on the back pages
of tailpipes in arias broader.

JUST HIT THE BALL AND RUN FAST

A dense cloud erased the world's glare,
sunny days and a few torturous months
from the coming seasons.

M is selling his card.
You chat.
It is difficult to overplant a valley in grass.

You are surprised by the bold bird:
a happy jab, a simple ouch
and a jumpstart before advancing.

LESS CONCRETE MORE REBAR

Oh we twisted it a good 1000 times 4
or more and found that there
is a bitter incentive these days
to outsource even a plate of dog food.

The main draw is no more than a proposal
thrown to the parasites.
It will be forwarded to me.
My nerves are fine.

One can collapse into a pile at any moment.
Yesterday it happened on the 6 train.
In the video
I have enough motivation.

In my splinter-free life
I am wireless
with no support for my legs and feet.
It is a special fate.

METHODS FOR CURING THE SOUL

People love drama,
invented purpose
and invisible technology.

Fred skipped dinner and a bug fix
enabling him to open
in a slightly higher gear.

A young woman wept
restructuring her emotions
to stabilize an inner band of rain.

It is Saturday
a fine day
for a spacewalk.

LISTENING ASTRIDE

One with the radio
and feeling the interference
shaking the infinite woof

I adjusted the threshold value
dishing up a jumbled tradeoff
with reduced hum and buzz.

The band maintained a hilarious tempo
until Ann, raised by the mass
to an auxiliary factor *z*,
daintily tumbled up.

A statue depicted her flexing shadow
perhaps overdramatically
depending on the extent
to which Sally sang a clear case.

After hearing the last bond delaminate
the camerawoman said,
a tight mess is really attractive.

ガールフレンド
(GARUFURENDO)

Full of winter air
you blow on the night sky
and gulp the scope of the conquest.

It is common sense, that's all,
and bodes well
since Mondays are colored matched.

Breathing argon, you retie all the lines
which, when placed upside down,
will flower.

As for the crash of the small robot
its panel measured a hard hit
and was smashed.

To disable the backlash
you whistle an etude
to your girlfriend's cat.

But seeing that the horse is down
and the elevator is up
you had better take the stairs.

RIDING THE AMERICAN ELK

The woman who ate your focus
clearly understood the thrill.
She digested your scanty image
and craved a slug of your wonder.

Imagine a camel classified
by the tooth of an ant.
You cleared that perception off the glass.
Now it is super-clean.

Tarred smooth and rung slowly
the fog rolled a semitone
into a lovely, distant circle
making many go to bed early.

Look at that.
You seized the dial of unsocial times
and blew out a happy announcement.
Thank you

CPSIA information can be obtained at www.ICGtesting.com
Printed in the USA
BVOW07s1819270114

343003BV00002B/8/P